THE LAST BARBECUE

Brett Neveu

BROADWAY PLAY PUBLISHING INC
New York
www.broadwayplaypublishing.com
info@broadwayplaypublishing.com

THE LAST BARBECUE
© Copyright 2007 by Brett Neveu

Cover art by Rich Sparks
First printing: September 2007
I S B N: 978-0-88145-352-2

Book design: Marie Donovan
Word processing: Microsoft Word
Typographic controls: Ventura Publisher
Typeface: Palatino
Printed and bound in the U S A

THE LAST BARBECUE was first presented by
The Asylum Theater, Las Vegas, NV from, 17-26
March 2000. The cast and creative contributors were:

TED ....Jim Williams
JAN .... Maggie Winn-Jones
BARRY .... Michael Horvath
TAMMY ....Jenny Bobal
KATHY ....Katherine Engelhard

Director ....Davey Marlin-Jones
Set design ....Marda Mann
Lighting design .... Joe Kendall
Stage management .... Thomasina Mandolfo

THE LAST BARBECUE was subsequently presented
by The Aardvark, Chicago, IL, from 1 September-15
October 2000. The cast and creative contributors were:

TED ....Don Blair
JAN ....Ann James
BARRY .... Matthew Brumlo
TAMMY .... Heather Graff
KATHY ....Ashley Bishop

Director ....Ann Filmer
Set & prop design .... W Shane Oman
Costume design ....Michelle Lynette Bush
Lighting design .... Kevin Heckman
Sound design .... Edward Reardon
Stage management .... Leila West Frazier

THE LAST BARBECUE was subsequently presented
by The 29th Street Rep, New York, NY from
18 September-13 October 2001. The cast and creative
contributors were:

TED . . . . Leo Farley
JAN . . . . .Barbara Myers
BARRY . . . . Peyton Thomas
TAMMY . . . . Moira MacDonald
KATHY . . . . Elizabeth Elkins

Director . . . . Tim Corcoran
Set design . . . . Steve Swenson
Sound design & original music . . . . Tim Cramer
Lighting design . . . . .Douglas Cox
Stage management . . . . Ceasar Malantic

SPECIAL THANKS

Ed Sobel, Ann Filmer, Ian Morgan, Russ Tutterow,
Chicago Dramatists, AROT, Jonathan Lomma,
and Chicago storefront theater.

CHARACTERS & SETTING

TED, *male, late fifties*
JAN, *female, late fifties*
BARRY, *male, twenty-eight*
TAMMY, *female, twenty-five*
KATHY, *female, twenty-eight*

Time: present—summer.

Place: the side yard between two houses in a medium sized town.

to Kristen and Lia Pearl

ACT ONE

(Lights up. The side yard of a house. A low chain-link fence separates two yards with an open space in front. A bird bath sits somewhere. A rose bush. An empty trellis)

(Enter TED. *He carries a lawn chair. He sets it up. He exits.)*

(A few beats)

*(*TED *re-enters. He has two other lawn chairs. He sets those up.)*

*(*TED *exits.)*

JAN: *(O S)* Ted? Ted? Did you bring the cooler up?

*(*TED *enters with a cooler. He sets it down.)*

JAN: *(Cont'd O S)* Ted?

*(*TED *exits.)*

JAN: *(Cont'd O S)* Ted? *(She enters. She looks at the cooler. She opens it. She looks inside. She closes the cooler.)* Ted? *(She exits.)*

(A few beats.)

*(*TED *enters with ice. He sets the ice next to the cooler.)*

*(*TED *exits.)*

JAN: *(Cont'd O S)* Ted? Should I call Michelle? I know she said two-thirty or three, but should I call her? *(She enters.)* Ted? *(She looks at bags of ice. She picks one bag up and tries to spill it into the cooler. Some of it does.)* Ted?

(She picks up some of the cubes and puts them in the cooler. She exits.)

(TED enters with some six packs of soda.)

(TED opens the cooler and puts them inside, putting the unopened bag of ice on top of the soda. He closes the cooler.)

(TED exits.)

JAN: *(Cont'd O S)* Ted?

TED: *(O S)* Yeah.

JAN: *(O S)* I'm going to call Michelle and see what time.

(TED re-enters with a medium sized grill. He pulls it over by the chairs and the cooler. He opens it. He shuts it. He sits.)

(A few beats.)

JAN: *(Cont'd O S)* Ted? I left a message because she wasn't home. I just told her we were setting up for two-thirty.

(TED opens the cooler. He takes out a soda. He opens the soda. He takes a sip or two.)

(JAN enters.)

JAN: Those aren't cold.

TED: I'm thirsty.

JAN: It isn't cold.

(JAN watches TED drink from the can of warm soda for a few beats.)

JAN: When is Barry coming?

TED: This afternoon.

JAN: What time?

TED: I don't know.

JAN: I should call him and find out what time.

TED: Does it matter?

JAN: I was just wondering.

TED: Three.

JAN: Oh. *(Pause)* We're starting at two-thirty.

TED: He might be early.

JAN: I should call him. *(Pause)* Did you start the grill?

TED: No.

JAN: When are you going to start it?

TED: Soon.

(JAN exits.)

(TED drinks some more of his soda.)

(JAN enters carrying a Frisbee.)

JAN: Do you think people will want to play Frisbee?

TED: There's not that many people coming.

JAN: You only need two people to play Frisbee.

TED: There's only going to be at the most five of us here.

JAN: I know. But some of us will be talking and if someone doesn't want to be a part of a conversation, they can play Frisbee.

TED: Two of them can play Frisbee.

JAN: That's what I meant. Barry and Tammy would maybe want to play Frisbee.

TED: They'll be dressed up.

JAN: Maybe we could all play croquet.

TED: All of us would have to play croquet.

JAN: Why?

TED: It's a group game.

JAN: We may want to play. Can you bring it up from downstairs?

TED: If people want to play, I'll bring it up.

(JAN *puts the Frisbee down.* JAN *exits.*)

(TED *stands and opens the grill. He looks into it*)

TED: *(To* JAN*)* I forgot to clean this thing.

(JAN *enters with some more soda.*)

JAN: I took these cold ones out of the fridge. *(She puts the soda in the cooler.)*

TED: Damnit.

JAN: What?

TED: This thing's not clean.

(JAN *looks inside the grill.*)

JAN: That's okay.

TED: Shit. Damnit.

(JAN *and* TED *stare into the grill for a few beats.*)

JAN: It's okay.

(TED *shuts the grill.*)

JAN: Everything's ready.

TED: Okay.

JAN: Is it too buggy?

TED: Out here?

JAN: Should I go and buy some citronella candles?

TED: Now?

JAN: I should go before she gets here.

TED: I need to start the coals.

JAN: Can you wait until I get back? *(Pause)* I'll be right back.

TED: Fine.

JAN: Michelle should be over. If she comes over before I get back, there's soda in the cooler or wine inside. Or beer.

TED: I know.

JAN: I just hate to think of Michelle sitting in that new house all by herself.

TED: She's fine.

JAN: I'm sure she is.

TED: She's fine.

JAN: This will be like last year.

TED: I hope not.

JAN: I don't mean just like it. I don't mean that. I mean better, but still outside.

TED: Maybe this year it'll be me.

JAN: That's not funny. Don't joke.

TED: You're the one that said it's like last year.

JAN: You know what I meant. I didn't mean anything.

TED: It doesn't matter.

JAN: It should be fine.

TED: I already mowed and I'm fine.

JAN: That's not funny.

TED: I'm not joking. I mowed and I'm fine.

JAN: It's just sad.

TED: It's fine.

JAN: It should be better. It'll be fun!

TED: Good. *(Pause)* I really should start the coals soon.

JAN: Oh.

TED: Don't lock the door. I don't have my keys.

JAN: I won't. Okay. I won't be gone long. *(She exits.)*

(TED opens the grill and picks at it.)

(TED shuts the grill and exits.)

(A few beats)

(BARRY and TAMMY enter. They are dressed up.)

BARRY: I like this shirt.

TAMMY: You look nice.

BARRY: I didn't want to look like a dipshit.

TAMMY: You look good. It's a nice shirt.

BARRY: I don't know. I bet most of the people will be wearing jeans and some sprint car shirt. But not me. I want to look nice.

TAMMY: You look great.

BARRY: I don't look like some asshole?

TAMMY: No.

BARRY: I like this shirt.

TAMMY: It's great.

(A few beats)

BARRY: Where is everybody?

TAMMY: We can't stay that long.

BARRY: Are they all inside? Who is coming to this thing, anyhow? I thought this was a big neighborhood thing.

TAMMY: I don't know.

BARRY: Huh. *(He goes inside.)*

(TAMMY *waits outside. She stands there.*)

(TED *enters. He has a beer.*)

TED: Hi.

TAMMY: We made it.

TED: Yep.

TAMMY: Were we supposed to bring something?

TED: I don't know.

TAMMY: We didn't know because we're going to Palmas and then to the reunion right after.

TED: So you don't want any of the food?

TAMMY: Barry didn't tell you?

TED: No.

TAMMY: That we're going out to eat?

TED: No.

TAMMY: Oh.

TED: What time are you leaving?

TAMMY: We're just stopping by.

(BARRY *enters. He has a Coke.*)

BARRY: Hey Dad.

TED: You guys aren't staying to eat?

BARRY: We're going out before the reunion.

TED: What the hell am I going to do?

BARRY: About what?

TED: All this food?

BARRY: Where are all your neighbors?

TED: Why?

BARRY: Isn't this a neighborhood thing?

TED: No. It's just Michelle and us and you two.

BARRY: Hm. *(A few beats)* Where's mom?

TED: Running an errand.

BARRY: What time are you starting?

TED: I don't know.

BARRY: What are you, waiting for Michelle?

TED: Your mom knows what's going on.

BARRY: I think this whole thing is weird.

TAMMY: It isn't either.

BARRY: It is.

TAMMY: It's not. *(To* TED*)* It's nice of you, I think.

TED: I don't know.

BARRY: How old was he? Sixty? Sixty five?

TAMMY: Barry.

BARRY: What was he doing in the middle of July mowing his lawn?

TAMMY: Everybody has to mow.

BARRY: The death mow. *(Laughs)*

TAMMY: Stop it.

TED: He was fifty four.

BARRY: He probably looked older all crumpled over.

TED: What?

TAMMY: I think it's nice of you.

(Pause)

TED: I'm going to go get the briquettes. *(He exits.)*

TAMMY: Are you going to start being an asshole again?

BARRY: What?

TAMMY: Like you were in high school. You were such an asshole in school, and now you're not. I want people to see the person you've become. You were sounding like the same asshole that people in high school thought was such a jerk.

BARRY: I'm sorry.

TAMMY: You've changed. You're not that person anymore.

BARRY: I was just having fun. I'm sorry.

TAMMY: You just sounded like such a jerk.

BARRY: I'm just looking forward to seeing people from high school.

TAMMY: I just want them to see how much you've changed. They'll see that you've changed a lot.

BARRY: I know.

TAMMY: I can see why people didn't like you back then very much.

BARRY: I had lots of friends.

TAMMY: They were scared of you.

BARRY: They were a bunch of assholes.

(TAMMY *stares at him.*)

BARRY: Okay.

(*A few beats*)

TAMMY: We can't stay here very long.

BARRY: We'll go soon. (*Pause*) I haven't seen most of those people since graduation day.

TAMMY: Yeah.

BARRY: I'm looking forward to seeing Kathy and everybody.

TAMMY: I think it's kind of exciting.

BARRY: I think Kathy's coming in from New York.

TAMMY: You told me.

BARRY: She works for some pharmaceutical company.

TAMMY: Oh.

BARRY: I heard that from Jim Shaver.

TAMMY: I bet people will be surprised that we got together.

BARRY: You're probably going to see Mark and David.

TAMMY: That was a long time ago.

BARRY: I'm looking forward to seeing all of those people and showing them how much I've changed.

TAMMY: You've changed so much.

BARRY: I've really calmed down.

TAMMY: Yeah.

BARRY: It'll be nice to see all of my friends.

TAMMY: Yeah.

BARRY: I haven't talked to them for a long time.

TAMMY: It'll be fun.

BARRY: It'll be interesting for people to see that we got together.

TAMMY: I guess.

BARRY: I think people will be surprised.

TAMMY: I'm not surprised.

BARRY: Good.

(Pause)

BARRY: How long does it take to get the fucking briquettes from the goddamn garage?

TAMMY: He'll be right back.

BARRY: I mean we come all the way over here to see my folks for this dumbass party and where the fuck are they? *(Pause)* Man!

(BARRY *picks up the Frisbee and throws it at* TAMMY.)

TAMMY: Ow!

BARRY: Shit. I'm sorry.

TAMMY: Why did you do that?

BARRY: *(Yelling towards the house)* DAD!

TED: *(O S)* What!

BARRY: What the hell is going on?!

TED: *(O S)* Ahhhh! *(He enters.)* I can't find the goddamn briquettes.

TAMMY: Oh.

TED: Your mom put them somewhere.

BARRY: Huh.

TED: She pulls this kind of crap all the time.

BARRY: Huh.

TAMMY: Barry could go get you some briquettes.

TED: No, no. They're here somewhere.

TAMMY: If you can't find them though, Barry could go get you some.

TED: You aren't even staying. It doesn't matter.

(BARRY *picks up the Frisbee.*)

TAMMY: We didn't bring anything.

TED: That's okay.

(BARRY *throws the Frisbee at* TED *and hits him with it.*)

TED: Shit! What the hell are you doing!?

BARRY: Nothing.

TED: Why the hell did you throw that?

BARRY: I thought we were playing.

TED: What?

BARRY: I thought we were playing Frisbee.

TAMMY: It's not funny, Barry.

BARRY: I'm not being funny.

TAMMY: Barry, why don't you go get some briquettes for the barbecue?

TED: I'll find them.

TAMMY: Please?

BARRY: Okay. After I get back we'll get going.

TAMMY: Okay.

(BARRY *exits.*)

(TED *sits down in a chair.*)

TAMMY:I wish we could stay for the barbecue.

TED: We'll have a lot left over.

TAMMY: Barry's really excited about the reunion. He's excited about seeing all of his friends.

TED: He hasn't seen those people in ten years.

TAMMY: He's really looking forward to it.

TED: Where's it at?

TAMMY: At the Legion Hall.

TED: Oh.

TAMMY: Kathy will be there. He's looking forward to seeing her.

TED: Kathy?

TAMMY: Yes. It should be exciting to see her. He's been talking about seeing her all week. He's been talking about seeing everyone.

TED: Huh.

TAMMY: It will be exciting because some of my old boyfriends might be there and then Kathy.

TED: Huh.

TAMMY: How are you?

TED: Oh, I don't know. Tired.

TAMMY: Well, it was nice of you to do this for your neighbor.

TED: Work is a pain.

TAMMY: Oh.

TED: It's really busy all the time. I have all of these dumb asses working for me and none of them know what the hell they're doing. I come in every day and they look at me like I'm some sort of information machine. There to give them information and hold their hands and show them what the hell their job is exactly. It's the biggest pain in the ass. It's wearing me out. I've never been so tired in my entire life. It's not like I'm sleepy. I'm just worn out.

TAMMY: Well, this barbecue should be relaxing.

TED: So far, it's been a pain.

(JAN *enters with a plastic bag of citronella candles.*)

JAN: Well, I went over to Drug Town and they were out, then I went over to People's, and they just had the small candles. I was going to buy a bunch of the small candles but I just thought that I could get a few of the larger candles and it would be cheaper. So, I went over to Power's and they had some, but they ended up being just as much as the bunch of little candles, but I bought them anyway. They should last longer than the small candles anyway. Is it buggy? Are you guys playing Frisbee? Where's Barry?

TED: Where's the briquettes?

JAN: In the garage.

TED: Where in the garage.

JAN: Let me go look for them. *(She exits opposite.)*

(TAMMY and TED sit for a moment.)

(TED exits toward house.)

(TAMMY sits for awhile. She stands and gets a soda out of the cooler. She sits again.)

(JAN enters with a bag of briquettes. She sets them by the grill.)

JAN: Hi there.

TAMMY: Hi.

JAN: Oh. Is that cold? I put some cold ones in there. You should have a cold one.

TAMMY: It must be one of the cold ones.

JAN: It's cold?

TAMMY: Yes.

JAN: Ted put some warm ones in there so I don't know.

TAMMY: It's cold. It was on the top.

JAN: Good. Are you hungry? Did you need some chips?

TAMMY: I'm fine.

JAN: Good.

TAMMY: Where were the briquettes?

JAN: Oh. Inside.

TAMMY: Barry went to get some because we couldn't find them.

JAN: Well, you guys can keep them. I'll pay him back for the briquettes when he comes back.

TAMMY: No, that's okay.

JAN: No, we'll just pay for them.

TAMMY: Barry should be right back.

JAN: What time are you going to the reunion?

TAMMY: We're going out to eat first so we're going soon.

JAN: You're not staying?

TAMMY: Barry was supposed to tell you.

JAN: Oh. Oh well. That's okay. Michelle should be here soon. Maybe you can come over tomorrow for lunch and we'll have leftovers then.

TAMMY: Okay.

JAN: Did you guys play Frisbee?

TAMMY: No.

JAN: What time are you leaving?

TAMMY: When Barry gets back with the briquettes.

JAN: Oh. Michelle didn't come yet?

TAMMY: I don't think so.

JAN: Did she call?

TAMMY: I don't know.

JAN: Maybe she called when you were all outside.

TAMMY: Maybe.

JAN: I'll go check the machine. (*She exits.*)

(TAMMY *drinks her soda.*)

(BARRY *enters with a bag of briquettes just like the bag that* JAN *put by the grill.*)

BARRY: Shit.

TAMMY: I'm sorry.

BARRY: Goddamn it. Where the hell were they?

TAMMY: Inside somewhere.

BARRY: Goddamn it.

TAMMY: Just put them in the garage.

(BARRY *begins to exit.*)

(JAN *enters.*)

JAN: Oh. We found them inside.

BARRY: I'm going to put these in the garage.

JAN: That's all right. You can keep that bag and I'll pay you for the briquettes.

BARRY: That's okay.

JAN: No. Here. Let me get some money. How much were they?

BARRY: Mom. Just keep them. Use them next time.

JAN: That's okay.

BARRY: Just let me put them in the garage.

JAN: You can get them later.

(BARRY *exits with bag toward the house.*)

JAN: Michelle didn't call yet. She must be running late. I tried to call her, but she wasn't home. I didn't leave a message again.

TAMMY: What time were you starting?

JAN: Oh, anytime. It was rather up in the air. Two-thirty.

TAMMY: We'll probably be going soon.

JAN: Where are you going to eat?

TAMMY: Palmas.

(BARRY *enters. He has charcoal dust on his shirt.*)

TAMMY: What is that on your shirt?

BARRY: Shit!

TAMMY: Oh, you got it on your shirt.

BARRY: Damnit! Goddamn briquettes! (*He exits back to the house.*) Great!

(TAMMY *exits towards the house.*)

(JAN *opens the cooler and feels the sodas to see if they're cold. She shuts the cooler.* JAN *exits towards the house.*)

(TED *enters with a beer. He sits in a chair. He drinks his beer.*)

(JAN *enters.*)

JAN: You can go ahead and start the coals.

TED: Barry isn't staying.

JAN: That's what Tammy said. They're going to Palmas.

TED: So I'm going to wait to start.

JAN: Shouldn't it be ready to go?

TED: I'm going to wait.

JAN: Okay.

TED: I was looking all over for those briquettes.

JAN: I know.

TED: Where did you hide them.

JAN: I didn't hide them.

TED: Where did you put them.

JAN: I just had them in the garage.

TED: You must have put them in a weird place.

JAN: They were by the door.

TED: How could they be by the door. I would have seen them there.

JAN: I don't know.

TED: Let me put them away next time.

JAN: Okay.

TED: I know where they go.

JAN: Okay.

TED: I know where to put them so I can find them.

JAN: Okay.

TED: They go there by the potting soil to the right of the door.

JAN: I'll let you do it next time.

TED: Just hand them to me and I'll put them exactly where I can find them. I mean, I was looking all over the fucking garage for them.

JAN: I'm sorry.

TED: Barry threw a Frisbee at me and then I couldn't find the briquettes. He was out here and I'm searching all over the garage like some blind asshole for the stupid briquettes and he's playing games, throwing crap at me. Next time, I'll put them away and I'll know exactly where to put them so that I don't have to go around and around the place looking for them. I mean, shit Jan. Tammy made him go buy some more briquettes. That's just stupid.

(TAMMY *and* BARRY *enter.* BARRY's *shirt is wet, most of the dust stain is gone.*)

BARRY: *(To* JAN*)* Can you still see it?

TED: Where did you put the briquettes?

BARRY: What?

TED: The briquettes you went and bought. Where did you put them?

BARRY: In the garage.

TED: Where in the garage.

BARRY: I don't know. In the garage.

TED: Did you put them by the door?

BARRY: I just put them in the garage.

TED: Well, the reason you had to go get briquettes is because they weren't in the right place.

TAMMY: They're fine in the garage.

BARRY: They're in the garage.

JAN: It looks like it came out. *(Pause)* We should set up the croquet.

TAMMY: We should actually get going.

BARRY: I'm not going yet with this wet shirt.

TAMMY: It looks okay.

BARRY: It looks like I'm a dumbass.

TAMMY: Do you want to run home and change?

BARRY: No! This is what I'm wearing to the reunion.

JAN: I think it looks fine. It should dry fine. Ted? Could you bring up the croquet set?

TED: We don't have enough people.

JAN: We'll just set it up in case anyone wants to play.

TED: These guys are leaving and then it'll be dark.

JAN: Well, we'll just set it up and see.

(A beat. TED gets up and exits towards house.)

JAN: Lawrence should be there tonight.

BARRY: Yep.

JAN: Are there a lot of people going?

BARRY: I don't know.

JAN: It should be fun. Is Kathy coming?

TAMMY: Barry's been talking about seeing her for a month now.

JAN: She should be there.

BARRY: It's at the crappy Legion Hall. All those old men will be there drinking.

JAN: Really?

BARRY: That's what I hear.

JAN: *(Laughs)* Oh! They'll be there and they won't know what's going on!

BARRY: We should have it somewhere else.

TAMMY: It should be nice to see Kathy.

BARRY: She's not *your* old girlfriend.

TAMMY: My old girlfriend?

BARRY: You know what I mean.

TAMMY: No, I don't.

BARRY: You're all excited to see her for some reason.

TAMMY: I'm not. It was just a long time ago. I want to see what she's like. I want to see what all those people are like now. All of your old friends, like Kathy.

BARRY: They're the same.

TAMMY: It's just going to be nice to see her. I didn't know her in high school and you were together back then, so it will just be nice to see her.

JAN: What time does the reunion start?

BARRY: *(To* TAMMY*)* It's just you're pissing me off.

TAMMY: *(To* JAN*)* It starts at eight.

BARRY: What time is Michelle getting here? When are you going to start this thing?

JAN: We're really just waiting on her.

BARRY: I think it's rude that she's so late.

JAN: It's okay.

BARRY: It's been a year.

JAN: It's okay.

BARRY: I mean, her husband shouldn't have been mowing the lawn.

JAN: He was getting it ready for the barbecue.

BARRY: So what.

JAN: It's okay. She'll be here soon.

TAMMY: It's really okay.

*(*TED *enters with a dusty croquet set.)*

JAN: Oh good.

TED: Here.

JAN: Barry, can you set it up?

BARRY: We don't have time to play.

TED: We don't have to play.

JAN: Maybe you can play half a game.

BARRY: We're going to go in a minute.

TED: They're leaving for dinner.

TAMMY: Barry, help your mother set up the set.

BARRY: Why?

TED: Do what you want.

BARRY: We're going soon.

TED: Then don't set it up.

BARRY: It doesn't matter either way. If we set it up or we don't set it up.

TED: It just doesn't make much sense to me.

TAMMY: We'll play a little before we go.

BARRY: We have to get there for dinner.

TAMMY: I know.

JAN: *(To* BARRY*)* Here. Help me set up.

BARRY: *(Pause)* Okay. *(He begins to take the croquet set off, away from the house.)*

JAN: Thank you.

*(*BARRY *exits, followed by* JAN. TED *sits.* TAMMY *sits. Setting up croquet sounds are heard O S.)*

TAMMY: We can play a little before we go.

TED: If you want.

TAMMY: We'll probably stay until Michelle comes.

TED: Okay.

TAMMY: It was nice to think of Michelle. I'm sure she is happy she has neighbors like you.

TED: This was Jan's idea.

TAMMY: He was only fifty four when her husband died, isn't that what you said?

TED: Yep.

TAMMY: That's too bad.

TED: It was.

TAMMY: Did you take him to the hospital?

TED: I called 9-1-1.

TAMMY: Oh.

TED: He was already dead in the yard.

TAMMY: Oh. He was dead before you found him.

TED: Maybe. He was lying on the ground when I found him.

TAMMY: He wasn't breathing?

TED: I don't know.

TAMMY: He was all bent up in the yard, then?

TED: The mower was hooked up under his arm like he tried to steady himself with it and it got caught. The mower was still running, but it was all tipped forward so you could see under the mower. You could see the blade spinning around.

TAMMY: You found him like that?

TED: I called 9-1-1.

TAMMY: That had to be awful for Michelle.

TED: I don't know.

TAMMY: I mean, to see that sort of thing. Your husband dead in your yard.

TED: We were all pretty rattled.

TAMMY: Did you go to the hospital with him?

TED: No. He was dead already.

TAMMY: I mean, for Michelle.

TED: No.

TAMMY: Did Jan?

TED: I don't remember.

TAMMY: Oh.

TED: We really didn't know them that well. I mean we had dinner with them once over here, but they had just moved in not too long before he died. We had a real nice time over here with them.

TAMMY: That's good.

TED: That's why we planned the barbecue.

TAMMY: Oh.

TED: We were going to have a barbecue together.

TAMMY: Oh.

TED: Because they were both nice.

TAMMY: Yeah.

TED: And he was in good shape. It's weird that he had a heart attack. He was in really good shape.

TAMMY: That is weird.

TED: He worked in the yard all the time.

TAMMY: Huh.

TED: He and Michelle would ride their bikes around the neighborhood.

TAMMY: That's weird that that should have happened then.

TED: Yeah.

TAMMY: It sounds like he should have been fine.

TED: I guess.

TAMMY: My dad has to watch his health.

TED: Oh.

TAMMY: He had to do one of those tests where you have to run on a treadmill for awhile and they check your heart rate. For awhile we were worried about him. That was a few years ago. He's pretty young for that sort of thing.

TED: Yeah.

TAMMY: You just have to be careful with what you do.

TED: I really feel about the same as I always have.

TAMMY: Good.

TED: I feel in about the same shape.

TAMMY: You have to be careful though. It can happen and you don't even feel bad.

TED: I feel fine.

TAMMY: You just have to be careful.

TED: I feel the same.

TAMMY: Good. *(Pause)* I hope the reunion's fun.

TED: Tonight?

TAMMY: Yeah. We've been looking forward to it.

TED: Oh.

TAMMY: I'm looking forward to seeing some people tonight. I think that it will be fun to see what has become of some of the people. I remember when I was in school looking at Barry's class and thinking that they were a group that I looked up to. They weren't mean or anything, at least some of them. Most of them were all right. They didn't chase too many freshman around at the homecoming game. Things like that. I thought they cared about first impressions and making a good example for the other classes to follow. Most of his class was nice.

TED: Barry and his friends were nice?

TAMMY: The class was nice. I'm sure they'll be nice tonight.

TED: Good.

TAMMY: My class was always getting into trouble.
I mean the whole class was getting into trouble with
the faculty. The class would be reprimanded over
and over. But I'm looking forward to Barry's reunion
tonight. It should be fun.

TED: There'll be a bunch of assholes there.

TAMMY: I don't know.

TED: I would never go to mine because it'd be full of
assholes.

TAMMY: It should be okay tonight.

TED: I would never go to mine.

TAMMY: We're looking forward to it.

TED: I don't know why.

TAMMY: It should be fun.

TED: I don't understand why anyone would go.

TAMMY: I'm looking forward to seeing what people are
doing now.

TED: If I had ever gone to any of mine, it'd be full of
losers. I know.

TAMMY: You never know.

TED: I'd say, "What a bunch of assholes!" and leave in
two seconds.

TAMMY: There's an open bar.

TED: Great. A bunch of drunk assholes.

TAMMY: It should be okay.

TED: What could anyone have done in ten years?

TAMMY: I don't know.

TED: How the hell are we going to play croquet?

TAMMY: I don't know.

TED: This is ridiculous!

(BARRY *and* JAN *enter after setting up croquet.* BARRY *has a croquet mallet.* BARRY'*s shirt is dirty again.*)

JAN: Okay!

TAMMY: *(To* BARRY*)* You got stuff on your shirt again.

BARRY: What? Shit! Goddamnit!

TAMMY:We should just go home and change before we go out.

BARRY: I wanted to wear this to the reunion! I planned on wearing this!

TED: Oh relax.

BARRY: What?

TED: Just relax and go home like she said.

BARRY: It was your croquet set that did this.

TED: So.

JAN: Um...

BARRY: What?

JAN: Ha...

BARRY: Where the hell is Michelle anyway?

TAMMY: We should just go.

JAN: I don't know where she is.

TED: Go change your shirt.

BARRY: I don't want to.

TED:Then wear that one.

BARRY: Is there a problem with me changing?

TED: Relax!

(BARRY *throws the mallet at* TED.)

TED: You have a problem today?

BARRY: Do you?

TED: Throwing shit at me? What's the problem?

BARRY: Where the hell's Michelle so we can start this barbecue?

JAN: She should be here any minute.

TAMMY: We should go.

BARRY: Okay.

TAMMY: Let's go.

TED: You should go.

BARRY: We're going to go.

JAN: It's okay.

BARRY: Bye.

JAN: Have fun.

TAMMY: Bye.

BARRY: Okay. Bye.

(BARRY *and* TAMMY *exit.)*

(A few beats)

JAN: I wonder where Michelle is.

TED: I don't know.

JAN: Should I call?

TED: Don't call.

JAN: It's okay.

TED: Don't call. Just leave it.

JAN: It's okay.

TED: Leave it. Sit down.

JAN: I'll call.

TED: Fine.

(JAN *exits towards house.*)

(TED *opens the cooler. He shuts the cooler.* TED *exits.*)

(*Fade to black*)

END OF ACT ONE

ACT TWO

(Lights up)

(Late the same night, the same side yard. The chairs and the grill are still out. The cooler is still out, and so is the Frisbee. A few beats. BARRY and KATHY enter.)

BARRY: The cooler's still out.

KATHY: Were your folks having a party?

BARRY: I can't believe they just left this thing sitting here.

KATHY: Is there beer in there?

BARRY: You want a beer?

KATHY: Sure.

BARRY: Okay. *(He opens the cooler. He pulls out two beers. They are dripping wet.)* It's a little warm.

KATHY: Thanks.

BARRY: I hope it's okay.

KATHY: It's fine.

BARRY: Hell, we've been drinking warm beer all night.

KATHY: That's true.

BARRY: I mean at the reunion they had warm beer.

KATHY: Yeah.

BARRY: I can't believe that I drank all of that warm beer!

KATHY: Yeah.

BARRY: But it was free, so what can you do. *(Pause)*
It's a nice night.

KATHY: Yeah.

BARRY: Are you getting bit up?

KATHY: No.

BARRY: I could light a citronella candle.

KATHY: I'm fine.

BARRY: Here. *(He exits towards house.)*

(A few beats.)

(BARRY enters with a citronella candle. He lights it.)

BARRY: Here. *(He puts the candle on the ground.)*
That should keep them away.

KATHY: Thanks.

BARRY: My mom got them for the barbecue. They had
a barbecue.

KATHY: Oh.

BARRY: You got into town last night?

KATHY: Yeah.

BARRY: And you're over at the Heartland?

KATHY: Yeah.

BARRY: That place is brand new.

KATHY: Today I just drove around looking at the town.

BARRY: Is it weird coming from New York and then
back here?

KATHY: It's strange.

BARRY: I think it would be strange.

KATHY: I really didn't know what to think.

BARRY: I think it has to be strange.

KATHY: I saw my therapist five times this past week.

BARRY: Oh.

KATHY: I didn't know what to think about this whole thing, so I got so worked up about being back, and so I kept calling my therapist and making appointments and trying to figure out why I was getting so nervous. I just kept thinking about it.

BARRY: It must be weird seeing everyone.

KATHY: I don't know.

BARRY: Are you hungry?

KATHY: Not really.

BARRY: Did you see the cheese and who knows what else over on that little table? I ate maybe one of those things. They were getting all sweaty just sitting out there by the bar. I thought maybe I was going to get sick! *(Pause)* Man, did you see Jason Yardly?

KATHY: Who?

BARRY: Jason Yardly. He looked different.

KATHY: Jason Yardly?

BARRY: Someone told me he was the hit of the reunion.

KATHY: What does that mean?

BARRY: He had changed so much that it was so weird.

KATHY: Oh.

BARRY: It's weird that I still live here and you live in New York.

KATHY: I just ended up there.

BARRY: I know. I should come out there sometime. I think that it would be different. I would like to see what it's like out there.

KATHY: It's okay.

BARRY: Do you like your job?

KATHY: Yeah.

BARRY: It would be so great to do what you do.

KATHY: I like it.

BARRY: A pharmaceutical rep.

KATHY: I'm busy.

BARRY: And you get to travel.

KATHY: Yeah.

BARRY: That's interesting.

KATHY: It's just something different.

BARRY: Did you see that guy dancing on the table?

KATHY: No.

BARRY: Tim Mortenson was dancing on the table.

KATHY: Oh.

BARRY: He was drunker than shit!

KATHY: I missed it.

BARRY: He nearly fell on his ass.

KATHY: I didn't see it.

BARRY: It was pretty ironic with you and Tammy and Mark and David and me all standing there talking! I didn't think that would ever happen.

KATHY: Why?

BARRY: Everything that has happened between all of us, and how things are now. It was strange that there we were all talking to each other.

KATHY: That was a long time ago.

BARRY: But it was weird how we were all talking like nothing ever happened.

KATHY: We're older now.

BARRY: But it was so intense. I mean all of those relationships and all of those different feelings. All of those good times.

KATHY: Oh.

BARRY: It was great to see most of those people. Some of them were still assholes. It's interesting how much most people haven't changed.

KATHY: It's only been ten years.

BARRY: You just said that it was a long time ago.

KATHY: That's true.

BARRY: It's interesting, isn't it?

KATHY: Everyone pretty much looked the same.

BARRY: I meant more than looks. Everyone treated each other the same.

KATHY: I don't know.

BARRY: They did.

KATHY: I feel I've changed.

BARRY: You look the same.

KATHY: I've changed some in ten years. Basically, I'm the same. But I've changed some.

BARRY: Jason Yardly changed. People thought he looked great.

KATHY: Did you talk to him?

BARRY: I'm glad *we're* talking.

KATHY: Did you think we wouldn't talk to each other?

BARRY: I wasn't sure.

KATHY: I had more of a problem just coming to town than seeing any one individual.

BARRY: Oh.

KATHY: And you're married.

BARRY: I've really calmed down since high school.

KATHY: Oh.

BARRY: I'm not such an asshole.

KATHY: You shouldn't be so hard on yourself.

BARRY: Oh.

KATHY: It's hard being here.

BARRY: Yeah.

KATHY: Being here made me feel so uptight. I would get so rigid.

BARRY: Everyone there seemed to be doing real well.

KATHY: I don't know. Some of them looked old.

BARRY: I guess.

KATHY: Some of them looked like shit.

BARRY: I guess so.

KATHY: I got cornered by Kim Norvell over by the bar and she started to ask me all kinds of questions. She first started saying how she lived in New York and how she didn't like it. She said she had lived right outside of the city and how it was just not something she could get used to, then she started talking about Omaha or something and then she practically started apologizing for living here now, because she lives here now with her husband and two kids, and then complaining at the same time about New York! She was wondering how I live there and saying that she would have lived there if she could have handled it but she is so glad to live here now. She didn't know why she would have thought she could have lived anywhere else. She loves it here. She completely freaked me out. I didn't know how to respond.

BARRY: Wow.

KATHY: I just didn't know what to say.

BARRY: That's weird.

KATHY: I really was speechless.

BARRY: Weird.

KATHY: Then she just walked away. She had this lost look in her eyes and she walked away.

BARRY: Kim Norvell.

KATHY: It might have been someone else.

BARRY: Oh.

KATHY: I don't know.

BARRY: Huh.

KATHY: I just feel weird about the whole thing.

BARRY: It was fun, though, wasn't it?

KATHY: I don't know.

BARRY: Where did you drive around today?

KATHY: Around the town.

BARRY: Did you go to Martin Park?

KATHY: No.

BARRY: They have a new waterslide complex over there. They tore out the old slide and put in a new one towards the back, then they put in new showers and then out in the pool they put in these table/sprinkler things that you can sit down at and get wet at the same time. So I guess if you're hot then you can sit there and cool off and you don't have to swim if you don't want to. It really looks nice. It looks much better than it used to.

KATHY: Great.

BARRY: They had some zoning problems and they had some problems with some of the old people who didn't want to change anything. They wanted it to be the same as when it was built. It looks so much better, I don't know what they were thinking.

KATHY: They probably went swimming there when they were younger.

BARRY: It used to smell like piss.

KATHY: Oh.

BARRY: In the shower stalls, people must have pissed in there for fifty years because the bricks smelled like piss. It was sick.

KATHY: I don't remember.

BARRY: We went there a few times.

KATHY: We did?

BARRY: We went swimming.

KATHY: Good.

BARRY: Good?

KATHY: I'm sure I'd remember going if I thought about it.

BARRY: John Pretzer was a lifeguard.

KATHY: I'm sure I'd remember.

BARRY: What kind of things do you do in New York?

KATHY: I don't know.

BARRY: There's enough to do.

KATHY: That's true.

BARRY: Do you go out to eat?

KATHY: Sometimes.

(Pause)

BARRY: Is your beer too warm?

KATHY: It's okay.

BARRY: I could get you a cold one out of the fridge if
you want.

KATHY: No.

BARRY: Okay.

(Pause)

KATHY: I noticed that the Big Bear closed.

BARRY: That closed five years ago.

KATHY: I used to get boots there.

BARRY: You did?

KATHY: These big rubber boots with buckles that would
get frozen. They had a weird gray felt lining and would
take hours to dry.

BARRY: That's so funny!

KATHY: I know! Isn't that funny?

BARRY: Yeah!

KATHY: My toes would get cold.

BARRY: I hate that.

KATHY: It was awful. I hated it.

BARRY: I hate that, too.

KATHY: It's too bad that the Big Bear closed.

BARRY: Yeah. Nollens closed. A few other places closed.

KATHY: Oh.

BARRY: Yeah.

KATHY: I think I'd like a cold beer now.

BARRY: Do you want a cold beer?

KATHY: Yes please.

BARRY: Okay. I'll be right back.

(BARRY *exits quickly towards the house. A few beats.*)

TED: *(O S)* Hello? *(He enters from the garage area. He's wearing jeans and a t-shirt. He doesn't wear any shoes.)*

(KATHY *sits there.*)

TED: Hello?

KATHY: Hi.

TED: Where's Barry?

KATHY: Inside.

TED: Hi Kathy.

KATHY: Hi.

TED: What are you doing out here?

KATHY: It's Ted.

TED: Right.

KATHY: I've had a hard time with peoples names tonight.

TED: You got mine.

KATHY: At the reunion, I kept doing that thing where you look at the person's name tag before you look them in the face. It was really embarrassing. I must've looked like the biggest jerk.

TED: Hm.

KATHY: You recognized me right away.

TED: You look the same.

KATHY: How are you?

TED: I'm fine.

KATHY: Good.

TED: It's late.

KATHY: It's not that late.

TED: It's been a long day.

KATHY: I know.

TED: What are you doing?

KATHY: Nothing.

(BARRY *enters with two beers.*)

TED: What are you doing?

BARRY: Dad.

TED: What are you doing?

BARRY: Nothing.

TED: What's going on?

BARRY: Nothing. We're just having a beer.

TED: Where's Tammy?

BARRY: Home. She left the reunion early.

TED: She left?

BARRY: She was tired so she left. I stayed.

TED: *(To* BARRY*)* Why aren't you home?

BARRY: We went for a walk.

TED: Why don't you go home.

BARRY: We're just sitting here.

TED: It's late.

BARRY: I know.

TED: Why don't you go home.

BARRY: We'll finish our beer then we'll go.

TED: Fine.

KATHY: Were you outside all day with the barbecue?

TED: Yes. I'm tired. I was asleep.

KATHY: I remember coming over here for barbecues.

BARRY: Good night, dad.

TED: *(To* KATHY*)* Oh.

KATHY: There was one time when you flipped out on one of those electric ice cream makers.

TED: What?

KATHY: Don't you remember that? You brought out this big old ice cream maker and some ice and some salt and some milk and you tried to make ice cream, but the ice cubes were too big or something and the thing on the inside wouldn't turn, so you started to hit the ice cream maker. You were hitting it on top, on top where the motor is and the thing it kept trying to turn and you kept cussing at it and started to pull ice out and you were throwing ice. You picked up the ice cream maker and you threw it out on the lawn and the ice and salt and milk landed and exploded all over. You were so mad!

BARRY: Good night, dad.

KATHY: It was sad and funny.

TED: I don't think it was either sad or funny.

KATHY: You really overreacted.

TED: It wasn't such a big deal.

BARRY: Who cares?

TED: *(To* KATHY*)* Why did you remember that?

KATHY: I don't know.

TED: Why would you recall that?

KATHY: It was just a weird situation. You threw an ice cream maker!

TED:Why bring it up?

KATHY: It was a barbecue.

TED: It wasn't a big deal.

BARRY: Is mom asleep?

TED: Yes.

BARRY: We're going to wake her up.

TED: It's late.

BARRY: That's what I'm saying. We'll wake her.

TED: Good night then.

BARRY: Good night.

(Pause)

TED: Leave.

BARRY: What?

TED: I'm not leaving until you do.

BARRY: Dad.

TED: Good night.

BARRY: Dad.

(A beat)

*(*TED *goes to the cooler. He opens it. He takes out a warm beer. He sits in a chair. He drinks his beer.)*

BARRY: Dad.

TED: What.

BARRY: This was a private conversation.

TED: You're sitting out on my lawn.

BARRY: So what.

TED: I was asleep.

BARRY: Then go back inside.

KATHY: I don't know anyone in town anymore. I talked to Amy Reiusswig at the reunion and she doesn't live here anymore. I think she lives in Illinois or Ohio. There were some people that lived here still that were at the reunion but I don't remember who they were.

TED: Oh.

KATHY: *(To* TED*)* Are you happy here?

TED: What?

KATHY: I was wondering if you're happy living here.

TED: It's late.

KATHY: I live in New York.

TED: I heard.

KATHY: It's weird coming back here.

TED: It's just a reunion.

KATHY: That's true.

TED: Then goodnight.

KATHY: How was your barbecue?

TED: Fine.

KATHY: Did you have a lot of people?

TED: No.

BARRY: It was a memorial barbecue.

KATHY: A what?

BARRY: A memorial barbecue for their dead neighbor.

TED: Good night, Barry.

BARRY: Their neighbor died mowing last year and so they decided to have a barbecue for him and his wife who still lives next door.

KATHY: That's shocking.

TED: It's not shocking.

KATHY: It's very shocking.

BARRY: This guy died right before last year's barbecue, so they thought it would be a good idea to have another one to remember him.

KATHY: That's nearly horrific.

TED: It's not either.

BARRY: What did Michelle say?

TED: She didn't say anything.

BARRY: She didn't say anything?

TED: No.

BARRY: Did she have fun?

TED: I don't know.

BARRY: Did you play croquet?

TED: Sure.

KATHY: You played croquet?

TED: Goodnight.

KATHY: That's strange.

TED: No, it's not.

KATHY: You all were just out here playing croquet on the spot where your neighbor died.

TED: We didn't play croquet.

KATHY: What a sad barbecue.

TED: It's wasn't sad.

BARRY: I think it's funny!

TED:It's not funny.

BARRY: I hope you all had fun at the memorial barbecue.

TED: Did you have fun with all the assholes at the reunion?

BARRY: Yes.

KATHY: We were all holding back from being assholes.

BARRY: I thought everyone was nice.

KATHY: I thought everyone wanted to kick everyone else's ass.

BARRY: It was fun.

KATHY: You almost kicked everyone's ass.

BARRY: What?

KATHY: You were just about to explode. Having to talk to all those people you hated.

BARRY: I didn't hate anyone.

TED: Sounds like fun.

BARRY: It was fine.

TED: You were probably the biggest asshole there. People were probably saying, "Shit! Here comes Barry! I don't want to talk to that asshole!"

BARRY: What?

KATHY: He looked like he was checking off names of people he'd like to hit.

BARRY: What are you talking about?

KATHY: You were like a robot that was programmed to shake hands and glare.

BARRY: Why are you saying that?

KATHY: It was funny!

TED: What an asshole.

BARRY: I wasn't like that.

KATHY: It was interesting.

BARRY: I had a good time.

KATHY: It was a moment in time.

BARRY: A moment in time?

KATHY: It was something that happened that will be like nothing else.

BARRY: It was a reunion. It was just for fun.

TED: It sounded like a real fun time.

BARRY: Goodnight, Dad.

TED: Relax.

BARRY: Goodnight.

KATHY: They had the same guy playing music that used to play music at the dances ten years ago. It was weird.

BARRY: Only the retards danced.

TED: The retards?

BARRY: They stood around dancing like muh muh muh muh. They looked fucking stupid. They hadn't changed one bit.

TED: How are they supposed to change?

BARRY: I don't know.

TED: How much have you changed?

BARRY: I have.

TED: Maybe you're the retarded one.

BARRY: I'm the retarded one?

TED: Except you're worse because you say you're a better person and that you've changed.

BARRY: I have changed.

TED: You're still an asshole.

BARRY: You're the asshole.

TED: I'm not the asshole making fun of retards.

BARRY: I'm not making fun of anyone.

TED: That's a nice shirt.

BARRY: This was a private conversation.

TED: Calm down.

BARRY: Just go on back inside.

KATHY: When I was driving around town today I saw this five year old kid carrying his dad's cigarettes around for him. When the dad wanted a cigarette he said something to his kid then the kid got one out for him. It really was a shame.

BARRY: What are you talking about?

KATHY: I just saw that today.

BARRY: What are you saying?

KATHY: In New York you see different things but you see different things here, too.

BARRY: What are you talking about?

KATHY: It's just different here.

BARRY: It's not that different.

KATHY: Yes it is.

BARRY: Not really.

KATHY: It's different.

BARRY: It's fine.

KATHY: I guess.

(JAN *enters. She is wearing the same clothes from earlier. She carries a flashlight, which is on.*)

JAN: Hello.

BARRY: Mom?

JAN: Yes?

BARRY: I thought you were inside.

JAN: No.

BARRY: *(To* TED*)* I thought you said she was asleep inside.

TED: She's not.

BARRY: I see that.

JAN: *(To* KATHY*)* Hi.

KATHY: Hello. Remember me?

JAN: Yes.

KATHY: Oh.

BARRY: *(To* JAN*)* What are you doing?

JAN: I was walking.

BARRY: *(To* TED*)* Why did you say she was inside?

TED: I don't know.

BARRY: *(To* JAN*)* What are you doing?

JAN: I said I was walking.

BARRY: Why?

JAN: *(To* TED*)* Are you waiting outside for me to get home?

BARRY: I thought you were inside.

JAN: I wasn't.

BARRY: What's going on?

JAN: Nothing. *(Pause. To* TED*)* Why are you outside?

TED: I'm having a beer.

(Pause)

JAN: Barry, could you pick up the croquet set?

BARRY: Now?

JAN: Yes. Someone could trip.

BARRY: It's dark.

*(*JAN *hands him the flashlight.)*

JAN: Thanks.

BARRY: Mom.

JAN: Thanks.

*(*BARRY *exits with flashlight.)*

JAN: Where's Tammy?

TED: At Barry's house.

JAN: *(To* KATHY*)* Hello.

KATHY: Hi.

JAN: Where's Tammy?

KATHY: She went home.

JAN: What are you doing?

KATHY: Nothing.

JAN: Kathy.

KATHY: Right.

JAN: What are you doing?

KATHY: I don't know. Talking.

JAN: You were all talking?

KATHY: Yes.

JAN: Oh.

KATHY: How are you?

JAN: Were you getting bit up?

KATHY: No.

JAN: You lit a citronella candle.

KATHY: Barry lit that.

JAN: Were you getting bit?

KATHY: No.

JAN: It's strange how they keep bugs away.

KATHY: I don't think there were any bugs.

JAN: They don't like the smell.

KATHY: Oh.

JAN: I read that in an article that they don't like the smell. It's a strange smell.

KATHY: I'm not used to bugs. I don't think I've been bit in years.

JAN: You haven't?

KATHY: No.

JAN: New York is like one big citronella candle, then. *(Laughs)*

KATHY: I guess.

JAN: New York has a strange smell. *(Laughs some more)*

KATHY: Or all the bugs just died.

JAN: They died?

KATHY: I don't know. The biting ones died.

JAN: Oh.

KATHY: Or something like that.

JAN: Where are you staying?

KATHY: At the Heartland.

JAN: It's new.

KATHY: It is new.

JAN: Do you like it?

KATHY: It's nice.

JAN: It must be different.

KATHY: It's okay.

JAN: *(To* TED*)* How long have you been waiting for me?

TED: I wasn't waiting.

JAN: I'm going inside now.

TED: Okay.

JAN: Good night.

KATHY: Good night.

JAN: I had a nice walk.

TED: Good.

JAN: Half the people's lights in the neighborhood are still on.

TED: Oh.

JAN: I wonder what's going on?

TED: They're just up.

JAN: I saw some people standing in their houses.

TED: It's the weekend.

JAN: I wonder if they were hot. They may have been trying to save on electricity by not turning on their air conditioning.

TED: I don't know.

JAN: Some people were out walking with flashlights.

TED: Oh.

JAN: Like I was.

TED: Yeah.

JAN: I just saw their flashlights.

TED: Oh.

JAN: They sometimes were blocks away and I just could see the beam.

TED: It's a nice night.

JAN: It's a gorgeous night.

TED: Yeah.

JAN: I'm going inside.

TED: Okay.

JAN: Good night.

TED: Bye.

(JAN *exits into the house.*)

TED: How long can it take to clean up the croquet?

KATHY: I don't know. It's dark.

(*Pause*)

TED: You didn't like the reunion?

KATHY: I don't know. Maybe.

TED: Oh.

KATHY: I wondered how it would make me feel, but I felt nothing.

TED: Did you notice that you missed anything?

KATHY: No.

TED: Did you notice you missed a few things that you had when you were younger?

KATHY: Actually, I haven't noticed much coming back.

TED: Oh.

KATHY: I looked at everything thinking that I would remember everything, but most I've forgotten.

TED: Oh.

KATHY: I would look at things and think that they would spark some memory. They didn't do that. I really thought that they would open up something from the past. But they didn't.

TED: You didn't notice anything at all?

KATHY: I noticed that most of the things around me I couldn't recall.

TED: That doesn't make any sense.

KATHY: I don't know.

TED: It doesn't.

KATHY: I must have had a summer job or something. Maybe the place where I worked has been demolished. I can't find a familiar house. I don't mean where I lived when I was young, but a house I went to when I was here. The layout of a friend's house. The backyard of someone's house. I spent a lot of time just driving around and I just don't know. It didn't do anything.

TED: I don't know.

KATHY: I barely remember spending time with Barry. I know who Barry is, but what we did I don't remember very well. There are times when I remember a few things, but they don't mean much. They're like old dry cake.

TED: That's too bad.

KATHY: I don't know. Maybe. It doesn't matter.

TED: Oh.

KATHY: It doesn't matter.

TED: Were you in the high school band?

KATHY: No. I don't think so.

TED: I was in the band.

KATHY: Oh.

TED: This may be hard to believe, but I was quite a trumpet player. I actually thought about being a professional on the trumpet. I played in a few bands and was in the army band. I used to enjoy playing to Barry when he was a baby. I'd set him up sitting in the couch, tucked in the corner, and I would play to him softly, I'd play a slow march you know like bah bah bah bah, and Barry, he'd look down and listen. He really enjoyed it. He was a beautiful audience. I really haven't played it in a long time. I thought about selling my trumpet a few times, but it's still there in my bedroom closet. Sometimes I think I'd like to wake up in the middle of the night, when no one's around and take it out of the case and come out here to the yard and play quietly. Like around two in the morning, two-thirty or something. With the lights off in every house in the neighborhood and just standing in the wet grass playing the trumpet. A musical fantasy right here. But fantasies are what they are. I have to tell you that there are more than a few fantasies that I have that stem from things I enjoyed doing in my youth that are now buried in the back of a closet. I mean, I think about things when it is late at night and I'm lying in bed and the neighbors lights are off and the grass is wet. There are lots of things to remember. I used to take women out and we'd lie down in the wet grass at two-thirty in the morning. I'm not saying I was a dog

when I was younger. I went out with some women.
We probably went to the same places that you did ten
years ago. Water tower hill. The church yard. I'm sure
it hasn't changed much. Those times are crystal clear
to me. Their wet skin pale blue in the starlight. But like
I said, there are lots of things I remember. In my mind,
nothing's changed. All that's the same. I haven't
changed. I'm the same person. I'm essentially the same.
I look the same. I feel the same. It's the same. It's still a
beautiful night. The stars are still so beautiful.

KATHY: Do you like jazz?

TED: No.

KATHY: I don't understand.

TED: I feel like I could just enjoy the night.

KATHY: Are you hitting on me?

TED: No.

KATHY: I don't understand.

TED: I'm the same.

(Pause)

KATHY: You know, I'm glad I moved away.

TED: Oh.

KATHY: You people here give me the creeps.

TED: Oh.

KATHY: What did you do?

TED: When?

KATHY: Did you do something?

TED: Our neighbor was supposed to come over for a
barbecue and she never came over.

KATHY: That's not what I mean.

TED: She didn't call or anything.

KATHY: Oh.

TED: Jan walked over to her house and knocked on the door and called her but she never showed up.

KATHY: Oh.

TED: I mean, we got all ready to have this thing and then we never did do it. I mowed the lawn and everything and we got all ready.

KATHY: Yep.

TED: So we just sat out here.

KATHY: I lived in Michigan for awhile.

TED: Oh.

KATHY: It wasn't much different.

TED: Oh.

KATHY: I lived there for two years.

TED: We have all this meat in the fridge and some salads and some buns.

KATHY: Oh.

TED: That's right. Piles of the shit.

KATHY: That's a shame.

TED: I know.

KATHY: It's a shame.

TED: I'll guess I'll freeze some of it and just take some for lunches until it rots.

KATHY: Okay.

TED: I don't think that I'll ever organize this kind of shitty deal again.

KATHY: Okay.

TED: This is just crap and no one even comes. It's a bunch of shit and no one even cares. I dragged this grill out and all this crap and it doesn't even matter. I could leave this thing out here on the lawn until the grass grows over it, I'd just mow around it and leave it here because it's a waste to try to keep it up. I'm never going to use this piece of fuck again. I'll just let it rust and die out here. I don't care. I doesn't matter. It can sink into the earth for all I care.

KATHY: Tell Barry I had to go.

TED: Oh. You're leaving?

KATHY: It's late. Like you said, it's late.

TED: Bye.

KATHY: Tell Barry bye.

(KATHY *exits away from house. A few beats)*

TED: *(To* BARRY*)* Barry!

BARRY: *(O S)* What!

TED: What's taking so long!

BARRY: *(O S)* What? *(He enters.)* What? Where's Mom?

TED: She went inside.

BARRY: This is a pain in the ass. Where's Kathy?

TED: She left.

BARRY: What?

TED: She left.

BARRY: When?

TED: I don't know.

BARRY: Shit. Damnit.

TED: You better finish cleaning up the croquet.

BARRY: I'll finish tomorrow.

TED: Maybe you should finish it now.

BARRY: Why didn't you tell me she was leaving?

TED: She was out here and she left.

BARRY: What did you fucking do.

TED: Nothing.

BARRY: You told her some crap.

TED: You should go home.

BARRY: We were talking and you told her some goddamn crap.

TED: I didn't even see her leave.

BARRY: Why did you say mom was home when she wasn't?

TED: I was just fucking with you.

BARRY: I'm not putting up with this shit.

TED: What shit?

BARRY: Listen. Fuck off.

TED: Nice.

BARRY: I was having a private conversation.

TED: It doesn't matter.

BARRY: It does matter.

TED: Nope.

BARRY: This is some shit.

TED: Nope.

BARRY: What the hell did you do? What did you say?

TED: Relax.

BARRY: No! I'm not going to relax. This time I'm not going to relax.

TED: Go home.

BARRY: What did you do?

TED: She thought you were an asshole.

BARRY: You did something! You said something!

TED: Finish picking up the croquet.

BARRY: No!

TED: Okay.

BARRY: SHUT UP!

TED: *(Pause)* Fine.

(JAN enters.)

JAN: Are you done?

BARRY: *(Pause)* Almost.

JAN: Did you have a nice time at dinner?

BARRY: Yes.

JAN: What did you have?

BARRY: Pasta.

JAN: What did Tammy have?

BARRY: Some pasta, too.

JAN: Was it all right?

BARRY: It was good.

JAN: Palmas is a nice restaurant.

BARRY: It was nice when we were there.

JAN: I like that restaurant.

BARRY: It was nice.

JAN: Did you see any of your old teachers at the reunion?

BARRY: There were no teachers there.

TED: Some of those people who are teachers now were teachers back when I was in school.

BARRY: Oh.

TED: Mister Stiles.

BARRY: Yep.

TED: Mrs Spiker.

BARRY: Yep.

TED: Mister Wagoner

BARRY: Yep.

TED: Mrs Herbolt died.

BARRY: I'm tired.

TED: It's late.

BARRY: I'm going to go.

JAN: Good night.

TED: Good night.

BARRY: Good night. *(He exits away from house.)*

(A few beats. JAN goes inside.)

(A few beats. TED exits.)

END OF PLAY

www.ingramcontent.com/pod-product-compliance
Lightning Source LLC
Chambersburg PA
CBHW070026110426
42741CB00034B/2637